AF610928

VERSE AND MORE

Verse and More

(from Sheffield)

Editha Morris

with illustrations by Rachel Lambert

Fulwood Books

Copyright © Editha Morris 2017
Illustrations © Rachel Lambert 2017
First published in 2017 by Fulwood Books
Badgers, Reeds Lane, Sayers Common, Hassocks, BN6 9JG

Distributed worldwide by Lightning Source

The right of Editha Morris to be identified as the author of the work has been asserted herein in accordance with the Copyright, Designs and Patents Act 1988.

All rights reserved. This book is sold subject to the condition that it shall not, by way of trade or otherwise, be lent, resold, hired out or otherwise circulated without the publisher's prior consent in any form of binding or cover other than that in which it is published and without a similar condition including this condition being imposed on the subsequent purchaser.

British Library Cataloguing in Publication Data
A catalogue record for this book is available from
the British Library

ISBN 978-0-9955747-0-0

Typeset by Amolibros, Milverton, Somerset
www.amolibros.com
This book production has been managed by Amolibros
Printed and bound by Lightning Source

Editha Morris

Of mixed Welsh, Irish and Silesian origin, Editha Morris was born in Derby in 1916; she had two sons: Adrian and Paul.

She started working as a beautician when the family moved to Sheffield in 1947; the family then lived successively in Broomhill, Crosspool and Fullwood (that area known as Hallam – Sheffield West). She continued working as a beautician and also teaching elocution, having obtained higher qualifications in both domains in London.

Amongst other things she was a member of the Hallamshire singers.

She later discovered her talent for poetry, these poems having been written between 1986 and 1988. Although very well spoken herself, she shows in her poems a talent for understanding and putting into words the way local Sheffield people speak.

A report in the *Derbyshire Evening Telegraph*, 10th January 1940 tells us: 'GOLD MEDAL ELOCUTION SUCCESS: At the recent examination of the London Incorporated Academy of Music Edith Lucas was successful in passing the gold medal examination with 106 marks.'

The Poems

2 Jan 1987
The Funeral Tea

I've just been to a funeral tea,
There were hordes of relations, the body and me.
I'd better tell story as if I'd just come
And then you will know them all – every one.
The deceased is Sam.
My name is Fred.
I'm a widower man.

My wife passed long ago – 'neath sod,
And left me on my tod.
We never had a child to rear
Perhaps as well, I fear.
For I was on the beer!
But we did have loved ones many,
Three cats, two dogs and Penny.
She were a budgie, a talking bird
But one cat ate her, then never a word.
Wife's funeral were a real right do,
And the funeral tea!!
Some spread wer't too.

This is Fred – me – and Sam was my friend
Now I am here, to follow his end.
There's Uncle Bob and Auntie Lil
Hadn't seen each other 'til
Many years had flown, and they,
Are happily greeting
Though, once, it's true, they did decide
Each other's company
They couldn't abide.
Martha and Harry met,
Filled with dismay
Glared at each other
And then turned away.

Can't quite remember –
Who was it pinched who,
But such an upheaval
The whole village knew.
Now they are there at Sam's funeral too.

But resentment's still there.
This feeling all through.
But not to worry, sad to be sure,
Now they are at it.
Tooth, nail and sharp claw,
Once it were true. She were comely and fair,
They were such true companions,
And much seemed to care.
Long in the tooth now,
One fat, and one spare.

Here's Bertie Belling,
He's boss-eyed, poor man.
Talk to him long, and your eyes cross – WHAM

Seems as if hammer is thumped in my back,
It's big fatsum Jessie, hit me with a smack,
And there by her side, tongue clackety clack
Is his old man, Jack
If he only knew,
What went on round his back,
Sitting in the shade of the old garden tree –
Dottie with Billie, with their three kids to see.
They weren't no closer to old Sam than me and he,
But I guess why they're here, like me – for free tea.

Fancy that now! Must have closed early,
Couldn't mistake her, with her red hair so curly.
It's Florrie and Will
She's skinny, he's burly,
Must have a word now,
Seeing as they're here
They keep the pub, the 'Nodding Sow'
And give a damned good beer
And do they sup!
Not half, I fear
Come the time to close the pub
Will can't see the lock
And bolts the plant tub

There's Molly the dolly,
With her husband Wally,
He keeps his cap on, for really he's bald
Get a kink, it is said
And he covers his head.
He has just one drink and his face goes bright red
By the way, he's good as a plumber
On his head the flies settle in summer,
In the winter his bald pate
Serves as ice rink to skate.

Then there's Mrs O'Grally,
She's the Post Office lady
Her husband does pensions, banking and such
She's a fund of all knowing
For always a-going,
To the folk around to gossip,
And pass time of day,
But if you're in doubt
And need owt, then shout
Through the grapevine
The P.O. will always help out;

There's three pubs in the village nigh
One's the 'Nodding Sow', just by
Another is the 'Singing Duck'
The villagers call it the 'Old Cluck Cluck'
The last renamed when the new folk moved in
From the 'Come in Now' to the 'Whistling Cow'.
So when it's just on opening time
We all say 'where to, is it now up!,
The Sow, the Duck, or 'Mooing Cow'?
We all have a good laugh,
For we know what'll be
Could be end of the night,
We've been in all *three*.

I see Mrs Moorly
Who always looks poorly,
Shouldn't much wonder if she'll go the next,
Finger on mouth!
Her husband's a case,
I tell you he's fierce rough and burly,
When he's up with his fists,
With a jump and a twist
I can tell you, and this is for sure,
Be the firm time of knowing,
You'd better get going,
Else you're out, cold as mutton on the floor.

I spot Olly Oat,
He does get my goat, With his shoving and pushing
Getting something for nowt,
In his hurry to pass me a few days ago,
I sure got my own back, and trod hard on his toe.
What a to-do!, when he trod on mine, too.

Now there's Dorothy Mallow,
Folk say she's so shallow.
Pity she's got such a large built-up boot,
For she looks very nice in her stylish black suit,
She never got married,
Seemed none came her way,
But I know it's different,
And could she make hay!!!
There's young Doctor Radley,
Call her if you badly.
Tell her and she'll come with a trot and a run,
She's always so busy,
Works hard til she's dizzy
And often, alack!
Meets herself coming back

There's Miss Mary Jones
And she's mighty clever
And though I do say it,
Good looking she be,
If owt ails your eyes,
Then with great skill, she tries
And when everything's dim you can see
A miracle worker!
She worked one for me!!

Now there's Janet Wood,
She would if she could,
She's never been able to keep up with Hazel.
Her sister is smart,

And she's very plain
But what's lacking in one,
Makes up for in brain.

My friend is called Ted
He called 'Come in Fred,
And have a pint while you're waiting.'
Then he said 'Thou'st cold, and thou'rt looking vexed,
If you're not ruddy careful, you'll be the next!'
I didn't like tone
He's like dog with a bone,
All I'm awaiting is tea, buns and ham,
I do wish they'd hurry up burying old Sam.

Now! Here comes Miss Mabel
Who sets each long table,
If it's task do, it's fine,
And the tea lasts a time,
She fixes the seats,
And displays all the eats,
And she treats them well
Those invited, and tell-
Does she, them squeezed
To park where they please;
I want a *good* seat,
Just here if I can –
Near meat, not the jam.
Now Sam is truly surely gone
The hearse is parked.

We set upon
The food to really have a feed
Don't cram mouth full for sin is greed
Sam would think this good, this spread
But Sam's not here, 'cos Sam is dead.

Talk about food!!

There were turkey and chicken,
A big side of beef
A ham neatly sliced
But I'm careful of teeth.

I can't stab picked onion,
With just one peg at front,
And the loose teeth at back
Will not take the brunt.

So, pickles and likewise I left these alone,
But then came the trifle and jelly and scones
There were soft drinks, and coffee and tea as you please
But we old-uns said *beer*
Then to take when at ease.

Well Sam's wife, old Minnie, did everyone proud,
All were refined, with 'please', 'pardon', not loud
Passing things round, not leaning to grab,
Oh I forgot! There were salmon and crab,
Minnie said, "Pity, Sam can't see the table,
What's spread out upon it"
But I've half a mind, if he did,
He'd be back on hearse's bonnet.

Arthur's pushed in, I reckon he's crazy,
He's married to Maisie
He helps on a farm
At least when he can
For the gossips and blathering
The village clan gatherings
Drive him often to drink,
Twice he's been plucked from the pub 'Nodding Sow',
Drunk as an owl, and landed in clink.

I mustn't forget this bit to tell,

The Vicar stood up and the proceedings went well,
At least it was good, all that was said,
'Til he turned two pages
And "She" 's what he read,

Then Sam's old brother, gave a loud shout
Sam's a 'he' not a 'she',
And gave Vicar a clout.
What a to-do, but all went so quiet
For bell started to toll
Put end to the riot

Then Minnie blew her nose,
Which shone brightest red,
For many the tears that day had she shed.
For Sam was 'Me husband',
She proudly did boast,
'He was always first up in morning
To burn breakfast toast.'
Oh me, oh my, Minnie,
Who allus wears pinny
This really has been
A good send off day.

I know he'll approve
When at last he can move,
Towards Heaven he'll be on his way,
I've had many teas,
Then sat at my ease,
But this day I really feel 'done up'.

With a farewell to Sam,
And another slice of ham
Did I hear someone say
'Hi Fred!, Come up.'
If it were friend Old Sam
I'll stay *here* if I can

Though it's time I went home
To my cottage alone,
And I wonder if I'll be the next un,

But if I should go
Who'll do tea for me? Flo?
No! She's gone before; reckon
They'll speak well of Fred?
Do they hear when they're *dead*?
Well! I'll know when they call '*Fred*' and beckon.

I've got indigestion, I scoffed food in haste
We all ate so much, it were like a Whit race.
I was full up in the end, and
Could hardly drink beer,
But I toasted old Sam in my mind as if t'were here.
We all shook hands later, with parson at door,
Sam's wife and the family
Wept just a bit more.

I then staggered home with me belly so full,
Then I sat with my slippers
Peered into the red coals
So cosy was I,
Reflecting on who'd do the tea when I die,

For I'm real alone, neither got kith nor kin
But I've always tagged on when funerals there's bin.
Now when it's time for me to get up and go,
And I leave my body
The old Fred that I know,
For I know I'll be me
Whatever folks say
Cos unless they believe this
They why do they pray?
And when I flap those feathery things
I think they grow, and they call them wings.
I'll ask the angels for a tow,

Because I won't have the wind,
To get off and go,
And I do believe, I heard if oft said,
They have a cord, think it's silvery or lead,
They hitch it to you, and then off do they fly
And you dangle behind like a cork in the sky.
I hope I'm not there arriving too late.
I understand from someone
They close gates at eight.
I'll stand and I'll knock,
And I'll say 'I'm alive now and dead.
Please Mr Saint, let me in – I'm old Fred.'
And then I can almost hear him say,
'Come in, laddo, we'll not turn you away.'

My word, old Fred, it's a long time you've bin
And I'll say 'Well it's all me. No repaired parts stitched in.'
'Come in, don't be scared.' And I'll say,
'Thanks, worshipful for giving the word.
There's one left, I know, down yonder, down there, I fear.'
We know Fred, Come in, your friends are all here.'
Inside, such a spread,
You never did see,
And you'll never guess this –
It were *my* funeral tea.

3 Jan 1987

The Corporation Seat

A Corporation Seat was placed across the road from "Wayside". It was put near to the bus shelter, and for the past few weeks, possibly youths, (with a sense of humour) have moved it here and there, (but nobody ever saw them do this.)

It seemed in the end this seat assumed a personality of its own. I did ask the office concerned to either fix it in the ground firmly or take it away altogether. Now (yesterday it has gone) I wrote the following:

There was a seat,
A seat there was,
And seemed this seat to ordinary be.
But amazing to relate,
This seat had quality.
For 'twas truly living, and –
So strange, for naught of this to see.

One moonlit night when all was quiet,
The Seat did up-end say,
"I think I'll walk a little while,"
It did, and 'twas found far away;
Brought to now where it should really rest.

It did for time, but full of zest,
It pranced about on wooden feet.
And Lo! It followed police on beat.
But alway in the morn, this !!!

Seat its meanderings wide didst range
And many a wearied mortal strove,
To bring it back each time it rose.

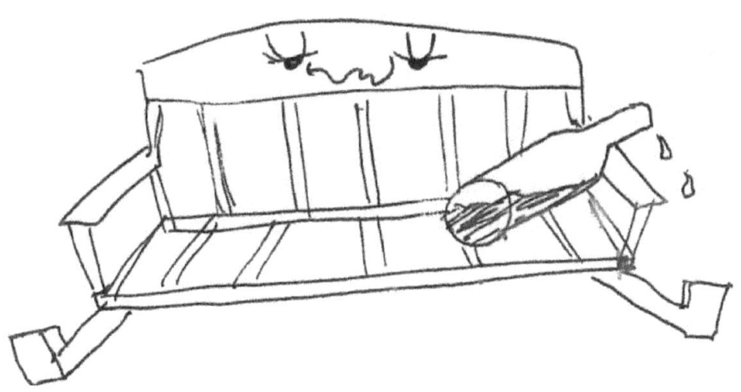

One day such a sight to see,
As that seat waved its legs in glee,
True it was the Christmas-tide,
And drinks in plenty were imbibed,
I swear that seat partook as well,
A drink or two, for o'er it fell.
Or maybe 'twas the rain from Heaven
But the seat *was* there,
But gone at eleven.

Surely to make its merry way,
Appearing sober, nearing day.
To stand in its accustomed place,
With a welcoming look on its wooden face.
One morn to sighs of great relief,
No seat to spy, but then belief
Turned to sorrow, for 'twas found.
In look,
Of calm contentment, seemed to yawn.
But off it went in early morn.
This time it crossed a busy road
And laughed and laughed, and said
"I'm blowed!"

And "I shall take off when *I* please
And those who want to sit, take ease
Must find an old seat to rest upon,
For my young life has just begun.

For *I* like change, and cannot stay
To hear the heavy bodies:
"Here's a seat, let's pause," and smile
But not for long just wait awhile.

"I am not an ordinary seat, for
I have style, and those who meet
To waste time in chatter long,
Makes me to squeak and burst in song.

Let them sit in bus shelter parked,
Close together, yak-a-yak
But as for *me*
I have to soon have change, you see.
And so I moved one little bit,
And those who saw this, had a fit.
Expressions on the faces around,
I swayed a bit more to astound,
And all who waited for the bus,
Tumbled on in fright, no fuss,
From the windows heads they shook
And looked again, for I was stuck.

Just my luck
Wedged in space
Nowhere near where I was placed
This I must have shuffled along,
When I rocked a big, and burst in song.
A funny thing, a bit crude I thought,
But standing near the seat, I thought,
"Did it speak?" I bent to hear.
A very pretty girl stood near.
A buxom lady too stood by.

The seat, despondent, gave a sigh.
"The larger ones I can't abide,
They fill me up, and hurt my sides."
I heard it say, "Come sit, come, come,
I don't want you, with your cushioned bum.
The pretty girl, so nice and thin,
So light to sit. Yes, my heart she'll win."

Come Christmas time, that seat was bored
And in the night when twas, it roared,
"Let me down it's cold I fear."
"Where?" "Just look up, I'm perched up here."
And there it was this seat of note

The whacking, tacking seat; nor gloat,
Did it now, for truly trapped
Out of reach, for looked as scrapped.
There it was on shelter roof
And then came ran, heaved down forsooth,
And now the place where it did stand
Is empty and no more to land.

Here and there, for now it's gone
To where delinquent seats are sent
And this is sad, the way it went,
We wonder if it will come back
It really should, with chains secure,
But do we want it any more?

But on the thought we wish it well!
We have had enough of it
To end as firewood, could be fit.
"So little seat, please keep away,
And give us peace, please, peace we pray.
Go and settle some place new
We need no seat, particularly *you*!"

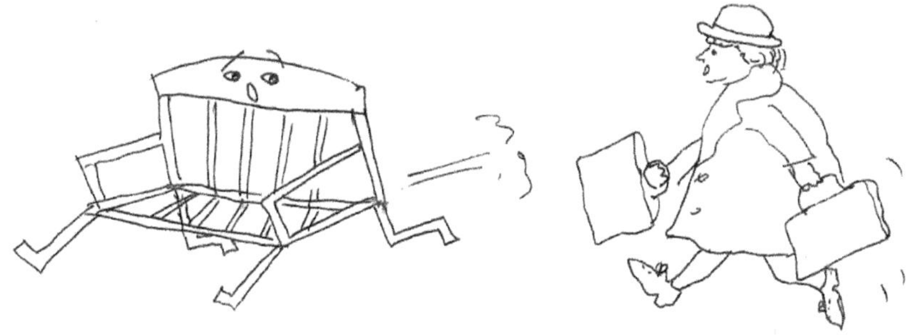

Dedicated to the Hallam Singers and Don Greenfield (conductor)

written after the concert on December 8th 1986.

There is a man called Don.
Whose reputation rests upon
His ability for good to be
At making music, teaching, he.

A dedicated worthy man,
Full of wit, and goodwill, can
By a look, from sharp blue eyes,
Quell whisperings, and much of noise.
And we do duly attention pay
To look, to learn, and little say.

Indeed if we do sing in "Hush"
And make of sound, when pause we must.
Helpful 'tis to have a push,
A dig from elbow sharp near us.
Don looks our way,
We docile being
Our all to him in voice to sing

We really want to please, and pray
We are in tune in perfect way
He notes when buried heads in books
And tells "Up please", eyes raised and "look".
So keen his prestige rests on this
A perfect choir! He's got his wish!!!

For not so we our own ways go.
We go Don's way at his say-so.
For nothing that we do can mar
The established fact, *We perfect are.*

Yes! We are the perfect choir,
Full of verve, and zest, and fire
To scale great heights to this aspire.

Now, in our finery 'tis the night
Like penguins clad in black and white
And so the concert to begin
And we in rows do shuffle in
Looking round to see who's next
For if you're wrong and out of step
Then sorely vexed.

Those who nudge, and looks convey
You are not popular, "Step *this* way."
On to the platform, or church seats
And those behind their necks do creak,
As back and forth like swaying reeds
To see Don's pointer, and "Come in" heed.

A mighty sound, the organ roared
And jerked awake, those seeming bored.
Endeavour we mouths open wide
To joyously sing like the on-coming tide
And just remember too, a while
In singing "look" and wear crooked smile.

The first part over, clap of hand
And there we bravely modestly stand
Then we sit, and then get up
And like as puppets on a string
We rise and sink, as birds on wing

Come the time, to look, to see
Whose in the audience known to we
Now in the 7th row I spy
A slight acquaintance Breathe a sigh.

Perhaps it's not so me she sees
For her eyes are crossed,
And she's hard to please.
Now she turns to one quite near,
And I do know what's said, I fear.
A nod of head "Just look that's her"
"Where?" "There"
"Didn't know that she could sing!"
"She can't – well – fair."

And now it is the turn to be
Of the audience, their glazed eyes see
They must bestir themselves and rise
So just imagine their surprise
When like as swallows in the sky,
We sing the descant loud with glee

We raise the roof with melody.
We skim and glide on upper notes
And pity those who growl in throats
Up and up we soar so high
And down we flutter like leaves to lie
The undercurrent of bass is such
Like thunder in the void of hush.

The concert o'er
Soon opened door.
But now the time to many praise
Who have worked well
And money raised
For goodwill flows
And off we file
In platform rows.
And let us not forget Don's kiss
For we've sung well, and bask in bliss
And like as babes at father's knee
We know Don's pleased, and so are we.

Now to Christmas 86
The year soon past
So fast! Alas!
The Hallam Singers gather here,
We know each other, but do we?
Mere members of a choral band
But in a way more – so we stand.

Joined in goodwill, friendship too
As this is well to follow through
So we come, and so we go.
Now with pleasure, all well fed
We soon depart to home and bed
To end, these words. My soliloquy!
We all do play life's symphony.

And when from this world we shall flee
To find the door, and turn the key
Travel through to surely meet
The ones we love in knowing greet
For in warm love they do belong
Then *Music*, *Light* and *Rapturous Song*.

The Hallam Singers went carolling
Written after this night 9th December 1986

To sing sweet carols in the night
And not a Blessed soul in sight
Only is it grey cats few,
All tinted with the moonlight hue.
And when we shrouded ones appear
The fur is raised
They flee in fear
Scurrying to their varied homes
And think no night is this to roam
Meowing loud, when at a door
"Let me in, don't shut me out
There are ghosts this night about.
And we do press thus on to sing
Of Christmas, and "The Blessed King."

But keen frost our feet do nip
And cold, stiff fingers books do grip.
Few things right in this cold night,
When few are out in this world of white.
Aspiring to bring merry cheer,
We visit flats so drab and drear,
And with the rendering loud to cheer.
We sing of the Babe, and His Mother, dear.
But where is the welcome voice bid, "Come in."
Only the television's loud sounding din
A barking dog, A desolate place
And not one door opened
Not *one* showed a face

On to the hospital, more worthwhile this,
For those laid low, their own folk will miss.
Milling around in group when we're there,

But this is a place where seems of good care.
We gather to begin, A few just hanging back
"Hurry there, quit gossiping,
For tongues do wag – Alack."

Now moving forward,
Off we go – step –
Down the long corridors
Seems endless, but let –
Nurse go ahead to show us the ward
And then we shall sing, and hope none will be bored

Sing we as walking, lustily with cheer
Those unseen, ill, do moan
Seem quite near!
'Spect they think they're now in Heaven
With such sweet singing, But it's only seven!
The last ward in there, pale and wan –
Those laid prone, no movement upon
But the hale and hearty in our midst,
With gusto sang with verve, and
didst not perceive the words they sang
Could not apply to those at hand.

"We wish you a merry Christmas"
We could probably speed them on
In fact one so pale
I felt she'd gone
If to sing it helped? "Yes" I'm sure it did,
But not to revelry and pudding "fig".
Hot tea, coffee, large mince pies
Quite a repast, good surprise.

Out into the night once more,
To enter in another door.
So to wend our weary way,
To the Old Folk's Home, and they
Shall truly be our last call.
For we're so tired, we've sung our all

This is cheery, bright the show,
And we assemble in a group, you know.
Half-way through, "the Faithful Come,"
Escorted by nurse "Can we pass please – run"
Modest whisper, "It's quite alright"
"Sorry dear, too much tea tonight"

Soon we're singing for our pleasure
Not for those 'old' now at leisure
Look we round, they all have gone
To sit in state, on the "Thingamy Jon".

So that's the end of carol going,
Let's hope we've set much "Goodwill" flowing
And enough's enough for this long day
Come hurry, let's be on our way
With open mouths we've sung our quotes,
And scoot off, home, with frogs in throats
Thankful to end all musical notes.

Come next Christmas, out into the night
And still not a soul, a Blessed soul in sight.

Written on January 16th 1987

The Haunted Pub

We fancied a holiday
My friend and me.
Did he think somewhere near, by the sea?
"Not on your Nellie, too cold now it be."
"What about one of them cheap trips abroad?"
"Not likely," said I, "With chit chat, I'm bored."

"Weekend break – All found and organised,
Easy, piece of cake"
"Let's try something different,
Away from noise, hub-bub."
And that's how we came to the little old pub.

We had heard about this,
Indeed it were famed
Supposedly haunted,
The "OO, AH" was named

The landlord was Bill,
His wife called "Our Cil,"
Priscilla, I suppose the name proper is.
Yes! It were so, Priscilla, he roared
Then they had a row, and up tempers soared.

We went for a weekend, a long one it be,
Friday to Monday, including the tea.
Left before that, in haste to get back,
For talk we have plenty, but courage we lack.

Though our living is hum-drum,
And complain much we do, (Alf and me!)
It was Heaven on earth to get home for our tea.

You'll know why when I tell you,
And calmed down I be.

Pub nice enough place –
Warm, and the face, welcoming of Bill,
We both supped a beer, then another to fill
Us with good cheer, and much of good will.
A holiday break with no wives to take,
And this we did say,
"Good to be here, enjoy every day."

Bright warm coal fire
But a quiet pub were this,
A bit more of company
Was my silent wish,
Not many that night,
Only locals a-supping,
Chatted with us,
Mostly about nothing.

Had a good meal,
Then off to bed,
Tired out I were
Soon laid down my head.
For not wishing to stay late,
I said I was weary,
"Talked enough" Alf, "I'm all in a dreary."
Don't really think to stay we'd be settled,
But in fact, Alf, he really was nettled.
When I said, "I'm off,"
"Too early," Alf scoffed.

"Time for another?"
"Nay! Call it a day."
Then off we went merrily,
And in bed we lay.
Something brushed by me
Must be a fly
"Bit late for insects," said Alf, closing eye.

He was in his bed nearest the wall,
And I in the other,
His, lest he fall
When his is merry, 'tis known he does turn,
Then out on his bottom,
On floor wedged in firm.

So we slept soundly.
As bugs in a rug,
Into the bedclothes right deep down we dug.
Woke the next morning as Lords, other's slaves,
For we felt refreshed, slept soundly as babes.

Oh, what a breakfast! A feast it sure be
And this was the first meal, Belly full when come tea,
"Slept well?" said Bill, his face gave a grin
"Aye Bill, t'was great, we settled well in.

Then Alf knocked my bed, as he got up in night,
And to tell you the truth, he gave me a fright."

"Nay lad," said Alf. "I did nowt of the sort.
It were you, who did make the clatter, I thought."
I said, "Drat him, to waken me up
A fine row there's been
Fell over his boots, and I heard a scream
Thought must have dreamt it
For tired out I'd been."

Alf heaved in bed
I heard him once more
Raising the roof, with crescendo in snore.
"I didn't get up," said Alf real annoyed,
As with his eggs, he ate little and toyed,
Appearing to be in deep thought it seemed,
Alfred was put out and and said
"T'was a dream."

"What," then said Landlord,
"Did something occur?"
"It did, said my pal, and frightened we were.
Door handle turned, and nowt did come in,
And Jim here was buried the covers within."
"Must have been the beer, lads"
Go out take a walk
When you come back have a drink
Then we'll have a good talk."

Come the next night, and settled we seemed
When something started moaning,
And the window did gleam,
With strange light,
That were kind of blue-green
I whispered, "Look Alf," "Now what? What's up?
Shut your eyes, close your ears, for Pete's sake, SHUT UP!"

Then a great thud, a bump "now what's that?"
"Eee, Jim, curtains did shake, and then they did flap."
Shadows appeared in the moon's eerie light
We shook with cold fright
Then came the tugging of pillows, our heads
Bumped on the springs of the bed wires instead.

The soft downy pillows, these floated round room
And we knew, Alf and I, this sure was our doom.
We felt chilled, the bedclothes had floated round bend
I thought of my bad ways
And vowed they would mend.
But by golly! Time's short.
And I'm *now* at my end.
Laughter so strange came round us in whirl
And we were nigh dead with our heads in a twirl

Dead beat at daybreak, we tottered down stairs
And met with the landlord, And his wife's icy stares.
"Say nowt, my lads," Bill said.

And wiped his face thrice
And Cil she did shudder
And hiccupped loud, twice.

"We have a ghost now," said Bill in a whisper
"He smothered a maid, and her lovely young sister
T'was on a dark night, A stranger appeared.
He were a queer one, and seemed mighty weird."
History repeats, it had happened before,
Two others were set on, and then many more.

"Spirits," they said, and none could deny.
Nothing was touched but the tenants did fly.
The landlord then told us the clock in the hall
Grandfather it is, about 6 feet tall,
"At midnight one night, the clock struck just 'one'
He fetched light and tools to see what had gone
He took front piece off, put his head well inside
Pendulum hit him, and he nearly died.
Strange to relate, the clock then struck "eight"
When it thought Bill had gone, it ticked proper then on."

We took the pub, it were named "Dew Drop Inn"
But as no one came near, the trade was so thin.
It's been quiet now for months, we re-named it to see
If you're frightened of "oo"
Could banished this be.
For as this pub is haunted,
The ghost could get tired, and leave us alone
For the staff left, never fired,
The "Ah" for relief that spooks have all gone.

But along came you two, and back now they've come
On your departure, perhaps we shall see
This pub, and its haunting quieted to be

We got our cases down the stairs
Alf's lips were moving, saying his prayers
Told me after, hoped that they
(the spooks that is) would stay away,
Not come home with us to stay!

Alf and I did go in haste. That pub's still there
Quick our departure, you never will know,
For we were quick off, and nothing to show.
That we had a weekend to give us a change
And nearly were smothered with ghostly hands – strange

Now we went wondering if we're haunted too
And the pub called the "OO-AH" that visiting we rue
Talk about things that go bump in the night
Gave us the willies and heart pains with fright.

My wife Beattie laughed it all off
Alf now is ill with shock and a cough
His wife Nellie, says she did know
We're always in trouble, wherever we go,
That damned pub may be called "OO AH"
But the distance between us, is not very far.

Moral

If you're ever going with a pal for a binge
Remember this story, and you'll really cringe
We're thankful to get home,
Safe with our wives,
And they may be a bit dull,
But we've escaped with our lives
Beattie and Nellie right worried they be;
For we go to bed, with a night light on
Since pub – Alf and me.

Written on January 1987

A Day by the Sea

It was decided that We,
That's the family and me (Ted),
Should gather together, (depending on weather!)
Off we should go (the whole lot you know)
For a day out go down to the sea
They all did agree, how nice it would be
The bus an' the train ride down to the sea-side.

So I told Aunt Fanny, and he sister Annie
Who's married to Ron
What about it?
We're on!!!
They told their daughter, (No better than she "oughter")
Who said with her boy friend she'd come, What fun!!!

My wife's name is Alice (keeps home like a palace)
Said we'd take our children, all three,
Their names: Maud, Harry and Bee
And then we did say to swell out our crowd
That we'd ask wife's brother, he's big and he's loud
He's Benjie, and his wife is called Mary Anne
They could bring baby and he's little Dan.

And who else? Mary's sister! So plain no one's kissed her.
She's Ellie, right pain in the neck.
They tried to get her off with Claudie the toff,
But nothing has come of it yet.

Now a ride, and the grub with ice cream in tubs,
A stretch in the sun, goodwill flowing – what fun!!!
Should please all the family, I say
Now I nearly forgot,
We've not got the lot

There's Gerald, and Ada?
With their toddler John
He's two, and so small,
Twice he's been nearly sat on.
Then there's the daughter,
Now 'spect they'll have brought her,
Her name is Joanna,
She plays the piano,
She sings, out of key,
The neighbours living round
Can't stomach the sound
They bang windows down
And they flee.

Now there's two in the family,
Who are very refined,
Their manners are perfect,
They're really most kind
It's Horace and Rita
She smiles when you meet her
No one could be sweeter
But the feeling is there,
She's not one to care,
Perhaps they won't come,
That'll please everyone.

Then friends said up street,
We're game to all meet,
Might as well join in the party
So then can we come?
And can I bring my Mum?
She can't walk very well,
But she's hearty

There's Derek and Gertie
Their Mum's Mrs Murphy.
Her husband took off with the woman next door

They are all very nice, but did ask the price
And we really don't feel we want any more
But what can you say when they're poor?
Then Grandma who's old said
"Well what about us?
We're very willing, let's come and no fuss."
We meant no offence,
So Grandma and Grandad did count up their pence
Gran's purse strings are tight
And there's many a fright
When it comes to the night
And she goes through his pockets
In glee, just for spite,
Then *is* there a fight!!!

Anyway, that's all the Clan,
If anyone else, they'll get in where they can
We'll part fill a bus,
For we're bit of a crush
Be cheaper to fill in the odd seats no fuss

If this way it's done
We can spend more on fun
After all this is our day
And it's only begun;
We all gathered together,
The early morn on,
For we'd booked the chara,
All vacant seats gone.

Yes! There were others going
But mostly our crowd,
And who travelled with us,
Would need earplugs, for loud,
Voices a chatting.
The kids milling round
The baby was screaming

And Ron lost a pound.
There were buckets and spades
A few skipping ropes
Plenty of swim gear
And several warm coats,

Could be a bit chilly
At this time of year.
But we're on our way
And the day's bright and clear
Baskets of eats, and vacuum flasks too.
But I'm telling you this
Not all of tea brew
There were plenty of beer,
And the cans were not few

Boxes were loaded
With goodness knows what,
I think if they could
They'd have brought baby's cot

Then we all milled in, fell in what seats we got
We all had a place? But Aunty Fanny had not.
She sat in the aisle, with her face in a knot.
Frowning and squinting, she looked very fierce,

And with her sharp eyes, her look could real pierce
Se there she sat, with not very good grace
The bus gave a lurch and she fell on her face!

She tried to get up! But was wedged in so tight
When she was pulled out, we changed places, that's *right*!

If you were thin, in the aisle you could fit
But if you were stout, there's no room for the kit.
T'were all quiet in bus, and peckish we were,
So we took down carrier bags, we'd packed with great care,
Handed food round, and silent all be,
As we munched and we drank, simply gallons of tea

Then a disturbance, a thud, such a slam
Case had come down, and hit head of *Sam*
Flattened his sunhat, and brought up a lump
Big as an egg cup, it were, such a thump.

When he felt better, a brandy he supped.
And this brought him round, into food well he tucked.
I forgot to say, Sam was up from our street,
Five children theirs, and decent to meet,
Another one due, I believe, yes! Next week.

The chara trip over, we gathered our things
Fell out on each other, and much laughter rings
The sun shone, warm, happily. And then it saw us,
Then went behind cloud, and wind came in sharp gusts.

We were spread out on beach, and nearly took in promenade
So far did we reach, deck chairs a plenty
The beach we moved on, but when we all poured on them,
not one, they'd all gone.

Then we opened food baskets, so hungry were we,
But Horace and Rita, went to cafe for their tea.
Said they discretely they fancied a treat
And a cloth on a table were more civilised than beach
And with their heads aching, a quiet seat out of reach.

We ate, and we ate, all fit to burst
Then we started on drinks, to quench our long thirst.
Kids were parked nearby, with their grub to scoff
If they were with us, they'd grab, scoff the lot.

Trouble broke out, and screams then were heard
"That's mine," "No it isn't" and then fists were bared.
In the "to do" young Harry did come crying and moaning
"Wow, what's now?" "Big Bud come, and took my bun."

All then calmed down and we settled to rest.
The young ones played ball and then trouble – "Pests"
Said Gerald to Ron. We'll move further away 'til they've done,
Ball then hit Ada, and bounced off her nose,
We collected the hankies for to stem if blood flows.
"Take her to First Aid." "Rubbish! She'll be alright."

A fly flew in John's eye, he yelled did, in fright,
Gran took her stockings off, and wiggled her toes,
Grandad took socks off and loud blew his nose.
Joanna went by with her head in the sky,
Not looking, kicked Grandad on his bunion, oh my!
He let out some swear words, and said he would die
But strange to relate, he recovered quite sharp
So quick on the mark when a swigful of brandy he got.
He drank all the lot, and looked for some more
But that's all he got.

Gran took off to paddle, walking gingerly on toes,
Her corsets did creak, whenever she rose.
The sea gave one look and rolled back in fright
At the spindly legs; and the hairy ones, white.

Poor Mrs Murphy then lost her shoe,
Hobbled about and what a to-do;
One lad had taken it off for a boat,
Put in near sandcastle in water called moat,
Sandcastle fell, the tide washed it down,
And then shoe had gone and never was found.

I said "oh dear!" and gave her my sock
To tie round her foot, but she really was cross
If you could have seen the way she could look
With the walk to the chara with a sock on one foot.

Now Annie thought that *she* would like to go down
For a bathe in the sea.
She disappeared then, appeared once again
Clad in a hand knitted suit, costume were white,
And *she* pretty sight, into the sea to swim round about
And ventured a bit further, a little way out.

Then she appeared on a wave, gave a shout.
"Look at me now"
We did, and good grief,
We wished she were hidden on a shelf or a reef
Must have lost bathe suit, "Get down Annie, please."
But she were so happy, bobbing at ease
"There's more of you showing than we really need!"

But still she pranced as a mermaid in glee
Looked back to shore and saw horror on we.
Seems knitted garment waterlogged be.
And 'twas not on the top, but caught around knee
We were discrete, when out she came sharp
Found the spot where her clothes she did park
Went behind rock, came out in her frock
Winked and said "Well, "I hope you won't tell!"

Benjie paddled in water, sneezed longer than oughter
And out came his teeth, where he stood.
We searched for them then in the mud
The tide then went out and we looked thereabout
And all in that part we did roam
And found them perched upon a stone.
A crab scuttled out, "What's this all about?"
Said he, when we moved his new home.

A young man said, "Madam, take your child away.
I can't take my pants off, for she's a nuisance I say.
She keeps lifting the flap of my tent, near the ground,
And when I've nothing on, *she*'s looking around."

Now it's half seven, time we're a going
It's starting to rain, and the wind cold is blowing
The sea's coming in, with the waves high aloft
And Grandma is cold, and starting to cough.
So we gathered our things, got kids and the lot
Traipsed on the prom, And found we'd lost John,
Then heard him bawling at top of voice loud
Found him at last, in another big crowd.

We then passed the Lifeboat and fishermen three
Yelled, "come for a trip on the Mermaid, all ye."
No thanks, we replied, we've enough of the sea
We've been by it, not on it, and we'll now let it be.

We got fish and chips to eat on our way,
And chocolates and biscuits to finish the day
The bus we fell on, now home we shall go
'Cept a stop for the toilets, a drink and blow.

We looked then for Granddad, he was carrying a handbag
He isn't peculiar, this we do know
But the bag's full of junk with a large household key
And it's heavy for Gran, with her rheumaticy knee.

We had a good sing, "Down the old bull and bush"
And after a journey, we're home. What a crush!!
And that is the story, A long one to tell
But it was a good time and all did go well
Now I believe you're as exhausted as me.
And that is the tale of "*A Day By the Sea*"

February 1986

A Birthday Treat

Now, what could we do for a birthday treat,
With the kids around and about up our street?
My son is Jamie, His sister – our Maisie
And Jamie will be seven on Friday March eleven
After all, seven to be is good and we
Decided perhaps a party at home,
Not such a good thing, Young ones apt to roam!
And neighbours complain of the noise, and the like
But mostly it's that kid next door, Mike, what a tyke.

There's no cause to upset folk, and important to know
That good relationship reign in *our* little row.
Well now, said we to our son, what do you think of a picnic?
That's fun!
But that didn't suit – for his look did convey
Anyone can go picnicking,
and day could be pouring with rain.

No! He didn't like that. "I don't want to go for a picnic, that's flat."
Well! What about a party to a pantomime show?
Jack and the Beanstalk is still on,
Left from Christmas you know
That then, we're settled, though Maisie right nettled.
Said it were kid's stuff and she wouldn't go.

She's nigh on *ten*, and her boyfriend is Ben
So with promise of a treat and plenty to eat,
And not a lot of little kids, short trousers and bibs,
She'd come – So that's done!!

Then duly we found, Jamie – long had asked around
And up to the present date –

kids numbered one hundred and eight
We said, far too many, cut it down, or we won't have any
So with much to-do, the list we waded through
And found the number right, and hoped the day were bright
He'd reckoned on ten, a few added on then
And Jack and the Beanstalk, had no clue, nor idea
What would happen in theatre when our lot should appear,

Ignorance is bliss, we've often been told
But a look in the future *can* give shivering willies with cold.
Fear and a feeling, what's going to be next?
We'd have cancelled the party if we'd thought "oo, too much"
With such a *bunch* of kids and such.

Well I must say the day were bright and clear
Everyone happy, all agreeing, all here
Two mums stayed to look after gear
And everything's fine, go off and never fear.

So we'd *go off* to the panto, another mum and me
With the kids to see the show, and come back for the tea.
The first knock on the door, it were Bobbie, aged four, With his mother Milly, right smart.

She'd never been wed – always reckoned that Fred
Hidden had a missus elsewhere.
But they made a good pair.
Though the milkmen went in for a "drink"
We all turned our heads but you can't help but think,
And Fred didn't know or a right row would blow
So we'd laugh with a nod and a blink.

Next to come Baxter and John
They are nice little boys
And they brought sweets and toys
They lived up the street,
And looked most clean and neat,
Their dad's a policeman on beat.

You could have knocked us flat with a feather
When he married twice-divorced Heather
Then little Sid with biscuits came.
He'd eaten most of them down in the lane.

Another big knock, and a new pair or socks
And Sid's three friends round the corner
Two girls and the lad name of Horner
They, the girls, were Hilda, and Ray.
Their brother was eight and he was called "Jake".

And he'd brought his blessed pet rabbit.
We said it could stay
We'd plenty of hay
In the shed at the bottom of garden
So in went the bunny,
It really was funny.
We'd already got a mouse
Complete with little house
Brought by Geoffrey who wasn't invited.

But as he had come, and just an extra one
And brought James a gun,
Well! What could we say?
He's so fat, weighs a ton,
"Oh!, it's you, love,
Yes, you can come"

There were Cedric and Bella
And young sister Ella
The little one came with the cat.
She put it on mat, but her Mum took it back
Mid screams and much stamping at that.

We all calmed her down,
And she soon lost her frown,
When chocolates and sweets were then handed around,

Then along came Tommy,
With his brother Donny
Oh they really were ducks, and so good,
They handed over parcel for all then to see,
And said "Where shall we sit, we're now hungry for tea?"

We said, "Not just yet,"
The show we must see,
Then we'd come back,
In *plenty* time for our tea;

Emma and Bobbie were asked to our treat
The family were veggies,
And didn't eat meat
But both brought large bags
To put in the eats,
And later were poorly with too many sweets.

Now from Mr Mickly,
(who always looks sickly),
Hired a mini bus at a cheap rate,
At two he'd collect us,
And then come and fetch us,
Himself and his very good mate.

We've got a privy at end of our path,
But the kids were so many
It were bit of a laugh,
The woman next door said,
"You're crowded out, see!
So come and use mine,
If it's only a *wee.*"
Thought better get this over and done,
We didn't want them to be up and down
When music were starting and show just begun.

Into the bus much excitement as well,
First in the queue, doors opened and fell,
Out all the kids, to tear up the stairs,
Pushing and shoving, like a horde of wild bears.
We were in *Gods* at the top
And sat on front row,
Could see over the ledge
At the posh folk below.

There were plenty of children
So noise didn't matter
But when curtain went up,
A hush! n'ere a clatter!

Now I sat at one end,
Milly at t'other,
Children were in middle,
Thought it all a giggle,
Each had a choc bar
And we said, "Ice cream to come."

We thought that would keep them quiet
When the show had just begun.
I thought I'd have drink of tea from my flask,
To give me strength while performance did last.

The band came in,
Music started to play
The curtain went up,
And so did my cup,
And wet were I then
Right to the end.
And through to my knickers the warm tea did go
And not very nice, I can tell you, *I know!*

Now show were on,
And all eyes upon –
The colours, the dancers,
Then Hilda sat on –
Geoffrey's big Mars bar,
All sticky it were,
Hilda did cry and Geoff pulled her hair.

Then with clapping and jumping
And saying "What's up?"
He dropped his ice cornet
And took one look,
Soon there were a loud voice roared from below.
"If anything more drops, we're *off*, best to go."
I did spit on my hanky to clean Hilda's frock,
Then there were trouble, the row ran amok,

Sid had brought his mouse, and fast it did go,
Up a woman's silk stocking
And out shoe's peep toe.
Sid moved then quickly,
Seemed completed unmoved,
Managed to catch pet,
And slipped him in trews.

I gave him a safety pin,
And we all felt secure,
But wondered what next,
And who else be vexed?
Bobbie knocked his bricks over the balcony ledge
They landed on a man's bald pate,
And bounced off a curly head.

Then back to the play,
Will shouted with glee,
Look out Jack lad, he'll eat thee for tea,
Jack turned his head,
And giant came with big tread,
Jack fell over beanstalk
And then hit his head,

Sid then cried, "*There*'s Widder Twanky
She's got a big bonnet."
Here comes the giant, with a big prop
Stuck legs upon it
The beanstalk so big
Giant's hair caught in twig
And beanstalk did sway.
Kids called "Call it a day"

Boom, bank went the band
To drown all the clatter,
And Widow Twanky lost her key
And giant roared at her.

The kids laughed, yelled and squealed,
As if let loose in a field,
I lost my hat, got a thump in my back
Said the folk from behind,
"If you'd go, it'll be kind.
We came to see Jack
But we want money back
It's been like Casey's Court,
With *this* mob you've brought."
The lady did come with big flashlight,
And shone the beam on our crowd,
I said *I* were in charge of the lot,
She said, "Missus a handful you've got
But if they don't sit and keep quiet,
You'll all have to go." I do say

There's more uproar here,
Than's made it quite clear
Than I've seen for many a day,
Music is drowned and bandsmen won't play,
Jack's fighting with giant on the stage you can see,
The beanstalk fell over
And Jack's hurt his knee.

So we shut up the kids
Departed in haste.
Made sure we got mouse,
Wiped choc off Jake's face.
We found Johnnie's shoe,
Oh! What a to-do.

Bus were waiting, good to see,
We tumbled in and home for tea;
Back at the house, the two mums all ready
With a jolly good spread
Jellies, cream cakes, not bread.
The children all sat, and
When we said, "Go!"
They grabbed and they pushed,
And did eat fit to blow,
Like as balloon, t'were all put away;
And no crumbs for birds
At the end of *this* day.

I don't think, I reckon
They'd had no food for a week
And they ate so much, the young ones did sleep;
The tea were a rite treat
With a few clips on ear,
But for the most part it were "Duckie" and "Dear".

My husband then said
With pals out of bed,
(They were on night shift)
They'd go for a jar,
It wasn't so far,
To their pub called "The Swan"
(When the kids had all gone),
It were a nice little pub
They have plenty of grub,
But the placard on wall
Looked like, "Swan in the mud",
It were fixed up some time, on front it were stood
Yes! I right sure it were there fixed firm from year dot.

For Swan looked like an hen
And chickens, *the lot*.
But the landlord were new

Twice he'd been spliced,
But the ham there were good,
Really thick were each slice.

Then to finish the party
We passed parcel round
To the music on record,
It stopped quick to confound.
Emma held parcel and then wouldn't part,
She tugged and she pulled.
When Bobbie did shout,
"Give it to me" and gave her a clout,
Brown paper broke, the string then came off,
The sweets and the chocolates
Each child then did scoff.

They played other games
One were a "Bite the apple"
And then we had tickets
In hat for a raffle.
Baxter said he were good at the apple one.

John said he'd won
When they'd played game the same
Baxter bit John's nose instead of the apple
John hit him hard and made his teeth rattle.

Soon it were time for party to end,
And children collected and home did all wend.
Jamie did think the day went very well
And the presents he had he liked we could tell.
So off the bed and sleep tired and worn,
But to have a nice birthday,
Well! It's the date you were born.

Then we sat because husband and me,
And we were full we'd had birthday tea.

And we talked before his night shift work.
Before I look under the bed
To make sure no burglar there can lurk
And I said, "You know, duck, what?
I've been thinking
What a lot we've got!
We don't talk posh
Saying 'Beg Pardon', and 'Gosh'
We don't look around
With a peg on our nose
We've not very much money
But it'll do, food and clothes."

We've two happy kids
And they're growing up a treat
And our neighbours are something
Right friendly on street,
We owe nobody nowt,
And it brings lump to throat
When you look at yon garden
Coloured flowers there a-float
Boats on the pool in the park near the school

We're sensible in living,
Being careful, no fool –
Are you as husband
You sort things out well,
And I wouldn't change *you*
For no one, to tell.

So love, aren't we Blessed?
We work and we rest
And we've a good going on
Nothing to grieve for, when over we've gone
And there's many that have a lot less than us,
Plenty of money but no *love*, no fuss
It's a day like today

I feel, Bill, it's grand
A really good birthday,
It all went to plan.
I'm saying this now
And I've got my old man.

Perhaps others have only a dog, bird or cat.
But if it's something warm to *love*
Then it's not much seems that.
But this must be right if you feel good inside
And you do your best
With nothing to hide.
You feel you've achieved that little bit more,
When at last you can open the wonderful door.
"What door?" said Bill, looking perplexed.
"I'll tell you," I said, as I reached for my specs
I like to think it's a door you come in,
And when you die, it's a door you go out,
And that's what it's about
A visit to stay
When it's done, move away
And feel all the love to meet those that we know
Nothing to fear, when it's like that to go.

And when it's *you*
Or might be me
Not long to wait
And then it's We.
And such a party gathered,
So many to see
When the door opens wide
And we're safe, sound inside.

Several days after the last part of the above words were written I opened the small 150 year-old book of poems by Horatio Bonar DD and I read the following lines:

"Without, within is light, is light;
Around above, is love;
We enter to go out no more.
We raise the song, unsung before
We doff the sackcloth that we wore,
For all is joy above."

March 14th 1987 (written then)

Women's Guild

If you're at a loose end and time to be filled
What about joining a Women's Guild.
Have you been? Were you seen?
Or were you a shadow
Like wraith on a screen?
Are you tall? Are you small?
Are you fat or just thin.
Will you stay? Go away?
Of no consequence be,
For joining A Women's Guild,
Operation – just me.

And we now welcome a new member,
Now could it be you?
Stand up, now we see,
The member to be,
So you bob up to show
Yourself, for did go to
To find a warm group
Not fasten neck in a loop
Everyone looks askance when you speak.

And have you not learned
To the wall go the weak?
If voice be loud and shrill
Take the floor.
But whisper like mouse
And you're closed in the door.
"Oh, I'm so sorry, dear,
I really didn't see."
And she floats away
You're squashed like a flea.

Now tentatively creep
To view notice board
But elbowed aside
As specs on a cord
Observe the list and then owner is bored
And when you can see
All full, but if cancelled
Add then, can ye.

All sit,
The lady with hammer,
Oh, small this in hand
She raps on the table.
"Attention, please stand."
Once the throng departed elsewhere,
And just a few moments
To say a quiet prayer.
Sit once again,
To hear, read the minutes,
It sounds double Dutch
But there must be sense in it.

Mouthful of words, the last time to mark
Then more papers are gathered,
For Committee to park.
The Chairlady in question has swallowed a plum,
And now lodged in her throat, this now has become.

Now, before you desist,
If you think it amiss
I'll tell you what to beware of – it's *this*
When you go in what first do you see?
A miniature jumble sale?
Not so, this to be.
The saving of seats
That cronies have evolved,
And handbags, gloves, scarves.

These be in careful folds,
Labelling the places of who does sit where?
Oh, my dear! Move anything if you dare,
And then you are sunk in the depth of nightmare
Baleful looks, and lips do mutter,
Witchcraft abroad, and do they move clutter?
You're very lucky if you can sit,
For this is *mine*, or *hers*, to whit.
And when you park, Good Luck you decide,
For your on your backside parked right outside.

If you're in the inner set, then all will be fine,
The women all gathered, seem zombies in line,
They gossip, and look round.
Posture and mime.

Hammer bangs table,
Puts an end to the babel,

Now to arise separate leaders of groups
To join one of these, you daren't
baleful looks,
What then is there really to please?
For no one seems silently sitting at ease.

First Social Studies Lady reads from a sheet,
And folks at the back loudly mutter and preach.
A voice midst each other,
"Speak up, dear," my mother,
is hard of hearing
Then everyone's peering,
A chorus now chimes
'We've not heard for some time,
Don't speak dear, just mime,
For we can't hear a thing,
Then from the table the bell, ting, ting, ting.

The Arts and Crafts lady,
She's not so like me.
Looks tall, and she's spare
She's *seen*, cos she's there,
She wiggles her fingers,
She looks very tough
With sleeves pulled up from the cuffs,
Then she descends, sits once more on chair,
With the cryptic remark "I think what I've said is fair."
And I think it's the business of bossing she means.
For that's *that* and finished
Her mouth, thin, eyes gleam.

Then there's a motion
But what's it about
There's so much of muttering,
You'll not so find out!
"Now who will propose this motion to pass?"
A hand waves in middle,

"Your name?" well stuck fast!
The chairlady pauses with a "Lah" and a stare
She's forgotten her name!
Has she got one?
Who cares!!!!

"Now, who will second the motion?"
You take a deep breath,
But the large lady against you
Shoots her hand up, hits your chest.
And what did ***I*** say?
Well, I said of nothing
They've carried the day
And the large lady's puffing
Polite sound of whispering
Diaries fetched out
And now what!
Search me!
What's this all about?
A visit to a pottery!
Great hockey sticks! "What?"
And if you're lucky
You bring back a pot.
Or perhaps it's a library
To walk round to see?
And in clatter – tongue – wise
It's time for break – tea –
Or coffee – maybe
Up rise the throng as the billowing wave.
The hum then of voices –
As you, oh so brave – venture to speak of one little word.
But, oh me, oh my!
Do you hope to be heard,
You are a phantom, and don't forget that.

Here on their sufferance,
Alack, oh Alack.

Why did you come.
For companionship – see!
Is that what you hope for?
You're unlucky; for key,
To be of note.
Raise so your voice high,
And then find a coffee cup spilt,
As that one wafts by
A billowing mob, who haunt places so.
And be big fish in small ponds,
Wherever they go!

"Do you take sugar?"
Your mouth opens wide
Then she's gone with the sugar pot
And your left like hopeful bride.
Another one offers to sweeten your cup.
And another swishes it away before you can sup.
Tell em my dear, someone venture to speak
You're so surprised your knees have gone weak.
But before you can answer,
"My Dear", she has gone.
And you are alone
Feeling most sat upon.
"Are you going to the dinner?"
Oh! You've had your hair done!
Do they mean you!
No! Not yet begun
Friendly exchanges
For you have to be
Quite ancient before any speak
At least one hundred and three
About conversation!

Well! Do have a try
"With!" "Oh you don't say"!
"Oh really!"

"That's marvellous!"
"Oh My!"

You've run through the gamut of this and of that
Then it's as a steam roller
Passed over
You're *flat*.

Is there any time to have a good natter?
But, oh my dear, yourself you do flatter,
Don't forget now, you're a Towns Women Guilder,
The odds are against you,
Like an unemployed builder!

The old biddies gather,
In small groups to blather,
The younger ones merge in a throng.
You must be so poor
If no car at the door
When we have so many
At least there are four
And holidays abroad!
Well, we're going again,
Nothing in England to keep us!
Oh Spain!
We're flying next month.
And again we shall go
To our rich friends in Spain,
Always meet us, you know.

Rap, Rap, knocks the hammer.
The women then gather.
Sink in their seats.
Full of coffee, tea (eats) (Biscuits)
The highlight of evening,
The Speaker!
Poor man.

I can tell you he's doomed
Before he's begun
He looks most self-conscious
He twice clears his throat.
The gimlet eyes stare
His discomforture to gloat
He hopes his voice reaches
Those seated at back
For they are still talking
Yes, clackety-clack.
Please ladies, says one of the Committee, at length,
And a hush o'er crowd gathers
On expectancy bent.

Now he looks at the crowd and grows weaker
And I think he wishes he wasn't the speaker
As the glassy stares to daunt his own style,
Then does he give a placating smile.
With a "hum" and a "Ah"
He plunges in far,
To float on the waters of a negative throng,
To get on a wavelength, feeling confident and strong.
Now the talking's over
The screen is put at the front
To follow his talk, then interesting to see.
The slides he has brought
Now in order and sought,
Now again we must move
And chairs put to prove
All can see well.
And no further need to tell – but –
Oh my dear, you cannot sit there,
That seat is booked, and there is no seat spare
And there's still our friend Gwen
Who, when all said and done
She's still to come,
And I knew the most uncomplicated seat to sit.

Is right on the floor outside the rear door.
Then the Chairlady said,
Go right to the back –
If you can't see now
Well! That is *that*.

The lecture I understand, *is* "Birds of a Feather"
And, Birds in all weather!
But the only feather that I did see
Was on a member's hat
And large too, was she.

She sat bang in the front row
Obscuring the screen,
And we stuck at the back
Only guessed what was seen
Well now, he's really doing his best, poor man
What more can one do, the best that you can.
A thin lady now is starting to cough
It must have startled the birds

Because I think they flew off
Now that is the end of *that*.
And all the women dutifully clap
Now to be really charitable
And try to be kind,
Whilst the many *do* seem such a kind
There are in the dark night of nothing-to-share
A few pinpricks of light
The few who *do* care.

These are a pleasure and a blessing to meet,
Warm is the feeling,
And pleased then to greet.
But I must say Alas!
They are but a few,
And you don't often see them

For they're shadows like you.
And they cannot make up for the tedious many,
Who fill all the seats
And of room, leave not any.

Well, now I'm a fully fledged member!!
What an honour, I must really remember!
A true band of sisters you know, – so to speak.
But most are so strong, and boss those who are weak,
Though most it seems unevenly matched
And grudgingly give.
Others grab, and they snatch
And sometimes it's a free for all.
Though there's not much *free*,
But an abundance of *all*.

So for the last time, as I really despair,
And wish I did not let them tangle my hair
I dutifully tried a bit of friendly conversation.
A caring and warm sort of unassuming conservations
"I really think ..."
But no-one heard
It's like water at brink,
If you're pushed, in you sink
If you're heard, there's no answer
For who can you be?
Just merely a number in the T.W.G.
And there's so many cardboard figures.
Light a taper
And they go up as vapour,
Into the air, as mist then, *Not there*.

Now I attended the meetings
And stayed for a while
In the hope that something would come,
To make *all* worthwhile.
But if the winds in the East,

Then, winds in the North
And *no* warmth is there
To ever come forth
As soft balmy weather, –
Seems there is *Never*
Then what point to stand
In the icy blast to shiver?

And take, as do many
And you're left as the giver,
Your coat you must don,
And when you have gone,
You hasten away as darkness from light,
Alone to go home
But relieved to go out.

Away far from women,
Who mouth naught, and shout;
Parrots in throng,
Each do belong,
But to gain ought? Tis "Nay,"
And when that lot are friendly.
Dear Lord! That's the Day!!
The WG!! Is definitely *not for me.*
But if it so happens it's really your scene
Then "Bully for you" if you see what I mean?

March 19th

"To the Desired End"

Someone said to me tentatively,
"What would you like to be?
If you could choose to see?"
"I don't know," said I,
"Depends upon what you mean."
In my eye a very faint gleam,
Wishing to be famous,
Or conversely acquire, wonderful knowledge,
to this end aspire.

And then will be seen,
As someone of note
And could be a dream
To ponder o'er and gloat.
"Oh no," said my friend,
"*This* is not so, I'm saying what would you like when you go?"
"Go where?" said I, "I've no plans at this time,"
"Well, you don't exactly plan it,
It arrives in good time,"
I mean, "Do you want to be buried or cremated?"
(She seemed quite elated.)
"At the end, when you're dead?
And it's too late," she said.
"When you can't say a word,
And even if you can, you're not *heard*."
"And I think we should decide before in the hearse we ride.

Well! I thought and I did ponder,
When up you go, back yonder,
It doesn't really matter, if thieves don't take your parts
But I feel this most strongly,
Please, oh *please*, leave me my heart.

So I said upon reflection
And felt of no dejection
"I'll be buried somewhere in the garden green, *there*."

And as we were walking in the garden that morn,
I indicated the spot
Where t'would be nice
The Lawn?
Then thought of the many big feet
Traipsing 'pon my remains
And a seat
Then to be there, where lunch could have had
Not much reverence *then*, I thought,
And felt sad.
So, we walked around,
And looked at the ground,
Decided perhaps under the tree
Oh no! *That* never could be,
That was the resting place
Where we laid our cats, all three
And there wasn't really any room
For them, and me to share a tomb.

Perhaps near the gate,
Where the newsboy comes through
He always leaves it open
So there's quite a good view?
No! I've decided it's too public by far
Far better to rest
In cool shadow, to relax
Could the mourners at best.
What about near to the wall?
Well! I am rather tall.
And a bend in the coffin
Would not do at all.

Where else to go?
Just under the new paving.
Right there in the row,
But they'll have to come up
And will they go down?
"I'm not certain of that," said I, with a frown
For there's bound to be a lump
With the box in the ground.

Be put to rest in the garden by chair.
Then in the spring
Whoever sits just there
Can relax, and look at the flowers near their feet
At buttercups and daisies
Appearing so neat.

The breeze soft will sway
The bright yellow petals
And if someone you can't stand
Then send up stinging nettles.

Sometimes when you're buried
They say you come back
I'm really assured this is a fact.
So on a dark night
Think how grand it will be

To tap on a window
At midnight, Psst, it's me!
And if it should happen you give folk a fright
Then glide off, and come back
Another dark night.

Or perhaps moon is full
In its circlet – white orb
And you're fed up with resting
And the ghost in you's bored.
Then rise up from garden
In your floating gown of lace
And with a soft moan
Press on window your face.

Now the problem must rest
Whilst official permit is sought
For it's not much use planning
If all efforts come to naught;
So down to the town hall.
I hopefully made my way
And at the big desk
I inquired if I may
Be directed to the department
Where burials and the like
Are dealt with in order
No complicated disorder.

From there I was sent,
So on thus I went –
To the offices of name
And there the sign plain
"Births, marriages and Deaths".
Well! The first has gone past
The Second will be last,
The third the die is cast,
The problem now the *task*

Well! all must go hence,
But, I want in pence
To ascertain the *cost*
The service, where the plot?
And when that all is done,
And life anew begun
The great day gone and done
And all settled in will
I hope it's not too costly
When my dear ones
Get the bill,
And please, no tears to spill

Well, in did I go,
And they said, "Hello,"
I said, "Can you tell me,
To be buried in the garden?"
"Who?" Well! It's just *me*."
They didn't look unduly surprised
A peeping round glass window
A few eyebrows raised,
This strange creature! Their eyes did appraise,
Then they sent me on.
With a paper to see.
Where next I should be.

It was the Environmental Health place,
And I made my way there,
With a measured steady pace,
And the staff were most kind
And much help did I find
"Yes"! a few people have
Been buried when dead
In their own gardens.
But let it be said,
It's not very easy, and seems rather strange
But we'll help if we can

But it's out of our range
"Well!, that's what I want
If you see what I mean"
"Yes, two inspectors must call, – they're a team."
The Health and Town Planning
Will send inspectors two,

And make yourself plain
And they'll see what's to do.
And the plans could go through.

The day dawned their visit
T'was on a bright sunny day
And discussions on "Death"
Seemed most far away

I met them at the gate
Puzzled were they to relate
And said "Oh! How small,
We imagined a large estate."
There's really not much space
Looking hard at my face
Soon we were talking;
Most helpful were they,
They come in and sat down,
Information to say,
I gave them some tea,
And they sampled the cake
And then when we settled,
Suggestions did make

They were most respectful
Particularly when they knew
I tried to do good.
We walked and time flew
The health man did say
"I am so pleased I came"

The other agreed
And we used Christian names
But I wasn't much forward
In the plans for the plot
Particularly when I heard
The snags
Quite a lot!!
Then there was the drainage
For pipes run beneath
Each side of the garden
And criss-cross in brief
Very much trouble
If you block the flow
With an arm or a leg
Or the main part of you,
Could even cause flooding
And then not a clue
How to make good
Pipes, mud and you.

If you're dug up when settled
It really is grim
For then what's the use
If you're out on a limb?
Then said the Health man,
"Infectious disease perhaps then we *learn*
They dug up once more
Your remains then to burn."
Well! I wasn't on that
For if buried I be
I don't want disturbing
And in smoke
Have to flee!

The next drawback to settle
Was – neighbours must sign
At least twenty six of them

All at one time.
To say they agree
A body laid to rest.
Near their front windows,
"Oh my! What a pest!"
And how could a secret be kept reverent like
When everyone knew
And gossip is rife.

Then I thought to depart
Without trouble to any
And the fond dream I cherished,
Was one dream too many
So many drawbacks with the clauses I find
This burying business is a bit of a bind
Then I really did think
It was better by far
To be cremated with ashes in jar.
And good this so far
So this I agreed.

In fact come to think
I could still visit the place
In quietness, own pace
And in the misty spirit garb,
Haunt around, and pause in yard
And perhaps around the garden
I ghostly light I could thus glide

And still survey surroundings
Whilst the loved ones inside
And if in the process
Of haunting that night
I could inspect the premises
To see they keep them right
Now I feel and I do know
That in light hearted way

I am giving the impression
We all are stuck around for Aye.
This is not so
In my experience to know
You meet your loved ones when over you go
And all living is on
A rhythmical flow
But as on a train journey
Or car, it matters not
Still,
On to the destination
But stop off it you will
If time then to kill
And it doesn't really matter
If you stay where you pause,
When time right, and cause of the delay
Can afford pleasure.

And if you've left your bones
Return at your leisure,
They're not much use any more to you now
Except to aerate, the Soil
As a farmer with plough
The body not yours any more to toil
And the gardener is pleased
To have nutrients in soil
In the beginning indeed
It was taken on trust.

And now it's left
It will crumble to dust
But you are now of loved ones aware
And earthly doings of sadness and care
Now left behind
And this is truly so
Remember these words
Loved ones left – and let go.

Weep how you will
Indeed weep your fill
But distress and pain over
Only on earth is there sorrow and woe.

Now if you should wish to visit "Wayside"
And here in the garden for a moment to bide
That is, I mean, when I have now gone
Not buried, but cremated.
Garden – ashes upon.
And you know like me
Life still does go on.

Now just sit for a while
With a welcoming smile
Then perhaps you will hear
A very soft sigh
And maybe a speck of dust
Flies in your eye
A brushing by softly
A kiss felt – "Goodbye"
Until we next meet
For we will, *You and I.*

PS Editha is actually buried in Crosspool Cemetery, Sheffield, 900 feet up, with a splendid view of the Pennine Hills from her last resting place.

April 1987

Down to the market

"Have you been to our market?"
You haven't! Well now!
Perhaps you would like to go and look round?
It's mostly very crowded but folks are friendly I've found.
And there's lots that's amusing, and really I say,
It's a change to look about
On a big market day
.
Folks come from villages and places quite far
And the hustling and pushing!
If you haven't a car
You get that on the bus
And folks are all same
With the "Ta Luv", and "Yes duck",
Then you're warmed,
Glad you came.

So today, let's take bus
And travel without fuss
Take big shopping bags too.
And spare money we'll blow;
Now let's look for the bargains,
Cos the market's the place
And then everything's there
With time plenty to spare.
Well off we'll go then,
A cuppa have first,
Then we can bat on,
Having well quenched our thirst;
So "Bob's your Uncle", and if you're ready, Lil, let's go
Look! There's our bus,
And on time, what d'yer know!

In middle of morning,
We'll have a bite to eat,
And perhaps a cake too,
And finish off with a sweet.

Though really you know
I'm trying to slim
But you're a bit past that!
To start shedding weight now
I wouldn't call you *very* fat
That's Cathy "me-ow"
And really Lil, it's nice to be plump.

Though my Ned's only joking,
When he calls you a lump.
But if I got like you.
Well! I would be a sight
No offence meant if you've been slim.
Well! It's like trying to be smart
When you're big you can't win.
But you've got a big heart
And that's the main thing.
So buy pleated dresses,
And nothing to cling.

Well!! Lil really looked cross
I couldn't think why?
She clicked her lips twice,
And raised her eyes to the sky.
I did catch her look
I wasn't meant to see
For we've always been straight
My friend Lil and me.

On to the bus
We climbed the step high,
And looked round when on
To see who? Oh! Oh! My!
Another great friend
And relation to Lil.
She said, "Hi! You two."
To me: "You look ill!
Quite poorly and worn
I really think, Nell.
You should go home to bed
You're not looking well.

But you're looking champion
You really are, Lil."
And then they sat together
And gossiped their fill;
I looked for a seat
Had to sit at the back
While they were together, tongues clackety-clack!

But bloods thicker than water
And I felt quite sure
They were talking about me
When they nudged and with laughter
Each gave a loud roar.
Well! My back's broad
And I can *take* it, and still
She's always been my friend,
My pal, is old Lil.
Well! What do you know!!
We were there in good time,
The friend went elsewhere
She's a bit of a kind,
And we, Lil and me,
We did join the big crowd,
Swept were we in a huddle
With the crush, such a crowd
Voices! What noise –
Mums, and dads, girls and boys.
Kids squawking in pushchairs,
Some screaming with rage
Dummies shoved in mouths
Or sweets, chocs, in a daze

Lil nearly fell, over on old codger's stick,
I jerked on her arm
And pulled her up quick.
The woman behind said, "Fancy that"
Somebody pushed her and tilted her hat.
So now we're on our trip,
And have plenty of time
And the rain has now stopped
The sun's out and it's fine;

Now Lil's hubby's a drip
And he gives me the pip,
But he'll get his own tea

And butter him up, does she.
Mine is real easy like
Comes home on his bike
Could be quite early
And he's known as "Olly"

Now we're into the market
Through the heavy swing doors
I got a shove, and nearly hit the floor
Lil was fed up, someone trod on her toe,
She wanted to sit
But a push trolley caught her
And bruised her a bit.

So we took our time
Lingered at the first stall,
Fingered the produce
And a loud voice did call
"Lay off them, missus,
Them pears easy bruise."
We scooted off quick,
As if no time to lose.

We joined the next queue.
To take a bit home for tea
Saw 'Thighs, breasts and legs',
Gave a laugh; wondered which is best for me!

So settled on breasts,
Right good buy they were
Then off to the cheese stall,
To a row in queue there
If you're out of your turn
My!! Don't our ears burn.
"Get back, mum, play fair,"
And the looks, poisoned darts,
Shot straight at your heart,

You pretend it's a mistake,
And apologies loud make
But they sort of "cotton on",
And you're glad to be gone.

The cauli's looked good
I pulled one out to see
The whole lot collapsed
And Lil banged her knee,
We picked them all up (nearly)
But some rolled away
The stallholder shouted
"You're right clumsy clots,"
We said we were sorry
He said we were *not*.

I then bought a big one
To try to calm him down
But I think he charged double,
And snatched cash with a frown.

We paused at the flower stall
And my! What a show
All colours; could smell scent
All round there, you know
Lil said to me, it really makes you think
If you know what I *mean*
That the natural things in Nature,
Are fresh and they're clean;
"I say, Nell," said Lil,
When we then stopped to gaze,
"No wonder in church
They sing hymns to His praise."

I'm thinking just now
Of the one that we sang
When we went to Sunday School

And the harvest song *grand*
Then "All things bright and beautiful"
And there look you, see
We don't have to spend money to look
When so much is just free.

We made our way out then,
To the open market – when,
Dodging the raindrops
(It had started to pour)
We went out from the big market
Again got caught in *that door*.

Now stalls were open,
With canvas spread o'er,
Sort of coloured tents,
And it were good to see, for
No-one did shout if you picked up, put down
And the things you could get
For under half-a-crown,
Stalls crowded with shoes,
All colours and size,
And we lingered, Lil tried on,
And big were her eyes.

"Eee, kid, it's smashing,"
Like homing pigeons to go
Round the displays, we wish we'd brought Flo
She were another friend but seldom went out
Her husband's Big Harry
Was real quick to give clout.

Now, *shoes*!
We stood on one leg
Balancing best as you can
Like storks in a river,
When up came a man

Hang on to me, luv
I'll help you if I can.
He gave me a wink
But I'm partial, *I am*,
And he wasn't my type,
And he went off, and wham!
I'd tottered onto my bag
Which were there on the ground
And I *did* go a bump
And I then looked around,
I couldn't find Lil.

She called, "Cooee," I'm sat
Here, Nell, and look this is nice, don't you think?
She's put on a fur boa
And looked like a fink
I dragged her away

Cos I'd seen a hat
I put it on happily, she said, "Not that!"
It looks like a pork pie
Upon a white plate
What do you think of *that* for a mate?
I know that she meant unkindly to be,
Paying me back for remarks made at tea!!

Now it were time
(Real jiggered were we),
To get on the bus
And home for our tea.
With parcels and plastic bags
And shopping bag, *big*
Oh! And a jar of treacle,
Fixed on well *that* lid,
I wanted to make some parkin,
Ned's partial to that,
But I must keep slim
For I'd hate to be fat
Well! off the bus we got
Weighed down with our lot
Lil said, "Tarrah," and soon hobbled off.
She's not got very far
To carry all her stuff
So we waved goodbye,
And parted without fuss.

Soon I were home
Shoes off, cup of tea
Then I heard Ned coming
Opened door with the key

"Now Nell," he said, in cheery like way,
"Did you go to the market,
And enjoyed then the day?"
"Eee, I did, lad, and good it's been I must say;

The next time though, I really do think
I'll not go with Lil."
Said I with a blink,
"A lot of the time I spent looking round
Was for *her*, half the time
She were lost then and found,
So I'll go on my own
When comes next market day."

Then Ned said, "Look Nell,
What do you say?
If I come, makes a change
I'll see what's to *do*
What I can arrange
I'm owing a day, maybe it's two,
Then I'll take this off time."

Thought I, what a bind!!
"You can't Ned," I said, "I've my man friend to meet,"
(I meant it as joke) and he laughed all the week
"But," remarked Ned,
"Does he live up our street?"

He little did know,
Cos there'd be a fight
It were his best friend I were meeting
His name's Billy Wright!
Come market day next
If it's not raining, *fine*!
I'll be off to the market
To have a good time.

June 1987

The Treasure Hunt

"Oh my," said I, surveying the sky,
For we did have much heavy rainfall of late
And a look at the cloud
Could still be our fate
To have no fine weather
From now on to find
The summer that was
Wasn't much – a real bind.

Now what prompted this,
That you've just heard from me?
Is the fact that our choir,
Likes a party, and we
Endeavour to make
Before our long break
A get-all-together
And merry-like take
An outing or meal
Depends how we feel
And then when we begin
Our songs later on
Our throats are all rested
To throng platform upon.

Now the Committee of choir
Most worthy are they
And with heads bent together
Seems on business, all pray
Harmony may reign
And *that* they decide
Will carry the vote
And by *their* say abide

And all with enthusiasm were really a-fired
And the plan was a Treasure Hunt
To this we aspired

So to go out to a village
Castleton by name
And for its natural beauty
This village is famed.

So there to seek for treasure
On foot, I might add,
That is when we *got* there,
And were suitably clad.
Then when treasure we found
We'd all have a meal
At the Castle Inn or some such
Depending how we'd feel.
And if rain didn't fall
A pleasant trip for one and all.

So on the planned day early;
My friend came in her car
It were early evening
And a few miles, not too far
So we then all duly arrived
And others gathered there
Long sheets of paper given
And the clues were on them, where –
In varied ways to wander
And the seeking here and there
So into groups they got,
And I decided not
To be with no one special
To rather help the lot.

The wind began to blow,
And all traipsed high and low

And yet it was quite warm at that
As the thin ones strode well
But puffed those who were fat.

Now many deep in thought,
The rhymes for treasure sought
And mostly all looked happy,
Except me, deep in thought,
Perhaps I should join with that lot?

But they were not so keen,
And so I wandered off along
For crowds are not my scene!

Now let me see! O my!
Best look willing with a sigh,
I was *so* bored and gazed at sky,
Not much inspiration from there
And I didn't *really* care,
Let them who wish to wrack their brains,
And lost to view most were in lanes.

My friends in the car went missing
I passed a bloke asleep, though fishing.
Saw some of us
Tagged on at that,
And then I saw a big black cat
He meowed and I stroked him

And talked for a while.
The lady who owned him came out with a smile.
I then strolled along
A soft humming of song
There was no one in sight
So I lingered, then bright
Faces appeared around corner and *they*
Were still on the treasure hunt
I'd called it a day!
But I *tried* to show willing
And chatted away.
But nobody asked me
To help them to play!
Treasure hunting truly
It seemed a bit much
All this wandering and ambling
Well! One needed a crutch.
On these uneven cobbles
What was there to see?
Oh, some very pretty gardens.
So I stopped, flexed my knees.
Leaned on a wall,
And felt really at Peace
The chattering of my lot
Had passed on, did cease.

Then another few appeared
These truly absorbed.
Only it seemed to me

I the *only* one bored.
I decided to give them some help on the way;
But I saw an antique shop,
I paused, heard one say,
"Now what does *this* mean?"
Head bent over sheet,
So I skirted round tree,

And was not seen from street.

I had really lost interest
And walked a bit more
I forgot to tell this
Not far from the pub
A very deep barrel
Indeed a large tub,
It said in large letters
On a placard nearby
"Rest awhile here and stop"
And "Don't pass by".

But it looked very narrow
And if you were big
It crushed bones to a marrow
And if you were skinny
You'd be lost like a sparrow
But indeed I felt as I so often do
I start out with high hopes
But I haven't a clue.

Perhaps I am lacking in the social chit-chat,
But to tell you the truth, mostly folk talk through their hats.
In two minutes, I'm bored wherever I go
But now to the treasure hunt
What can I see?
A small boy with what appears a fur round his neck
Now what could it be?

A ferret no less.
I'd given up hope to ever find ought
And I fancied a rest, and sat down on that thought
Upon a stone wall,
But hard it became
I thought of the meal
And took courage again.

I stopped the small boy
To stroke of his ferret
But startled it were
And jumped then and ran
We looked here and there
It were catch if you can.
In a hunt of a sort
Not so for a treasure
But a ferret if caught.

To further my stroll my mind on this set
So from child and his pet
I wandered away
And was truly fed up and didn't want to stay;
I followed a few of *our* lot but they
heads down were engrossed, t'was a marvel to see
How absorbed one can get in such puzzling – not me!

Then we all gathered for a meal at the Inn.
It was called a sort of Castle
But it looked mighty small
And I marvelled it could hold all *our* lot at all.

Down some steep stairs
We trailed to behold
A very hot room
And small tables in rows,
All cramped together with narrow backed chairs
And if you'd long legs
You were best on the stairs.

Anyway, the meal! All the orders were lost
And what we'd all ordered
The landlord forgot.
While the staff sorted this out
Our boss woman did say
Now for the treasure hunt prizes, we may
Award those with the most marks.
A really good gift
And so theirs they got
The less bright did not
Then came the runners up.
I wasn't in any
But who cares, I might add
I'm not counted midst many

But a prize should be mine
For I did try, did I.
But my heart wasn't in it
And was pleased it were finished.
Then the plates came for each
And the manager called out
"If you recognise your grub,
Then signal and shout"
The dishes were varied
Yes! All mixed to see
And Margaret who planned it
Did shake at the knee
For truly *she* had her work out to find
Each one to pay for his eats
What a bind!

I found it hard on cramped seat to sit,
With my knees near my chin
And my mouth closed on bits
When it was over, we counted the cost
And gave them to Margaret, who was short.
Well! Her loss!!
And now at last, it's time to depart
And for future treasure hunts,
I've quite lost the heart
And as usual with such do's
I wonder why I've come
They all were *so* happy
With such jolly fun.

But me! Oh my feelings
Mixed, sad to relate
And I feel I am unique
And Chow – not my taste
Though really I must say
I enjoyed part of trip
But it were only a very small bit
It's really a fag to be part of a crowd
When they are so very noisy
And their voices are loud
So when I'm invited to join any bunch
Whether it's tea-time or dinner
Or just a snack lunch
It isn't at all what I really would choose
And when you're a loner
There's little to lose.
And if one withdraws from joining the many
Then there's not any friction, indeed seldom any
But with this treasure hunt
I suppose it's a good time
And the weather was warm
No rain, indeed *fine*.

But at the end when home is the goal
How rewarding to reach the last pole
As in a running race
The pause to get breath
And if you're in front
Well a little time to rest,
Home is the place a welcome to find
When the world is agin you, you are back with your kind.

Now I'm back, and sitting at ease
I realise how difficult it is to all please
I'm thinking too of the words now writ
I'm pondering deeply so I sit
And I'm thinking to how much does blend
With that of now and long since,
– wend
Do our paths in varied ways
And we speak now and then of the good old days
But life's a mixture of good and bad
Happiness and sorrows all to be had
Practice of a kind, when saying "All's fine"!
And flushing aside, the much wished not, bind
As you find many harsh words are said
And yet in life, easy the much that we dread
Try to feel happiness if it be hid
And move kindly midst others and of thyself rid
Unworthy thoughts
And so shall we find
The treasure in life
Is *Goodwill* to mankind!!

Into the Hallamshire Hospital

Went in Friday 7th August 1987 – came out the same day.
Went back on Sunday 9th Aug 1987, had op Monday,
Came out Thursday 13th August 1987
The following was written in parts during that period:

"The Ins and outs of Hospital"

Have you ever been to Hospital?
Well, that's the day!
For such an experience is unique,
And they
Those who do boast of the "ins and the outs"
Do really feel they are special no doubt
But as for "going in" so much will you know
Now of hospital life
If you should have to go
So now to my lot
It's for an eye op, I've got
Much am I confident –
The next minute I'm *not*!

So in to go
In trepidation and woe
Into the lifts, these go up to great heights
I went down in the depth
Cos no one was in sight
I pressed the wrong button
For the crowds had all gone
I'm now in the basement
Not *up*, to go on.

If you are lucky
Your friends take you in
Or better still cushioned

With kith and with kin.
They make it sure for courage to face
The unknown, the dragons,
(Thy mind runs apace)

Could swallowed be
In desperate fright
And smaller you grow
Like a babe in dark night,
Smaller and smaller
'Til you're a pin head
Going out feet first, toes up, for you're dead.

At least that looms the prospect,
A coward you be.
But where are courage and strength
It's all fled from me!!

Now into *this* lift
And upward you're bound
To be shot up and with a jerk
Then the ward to be found.
The nurse who's in charge
Sit you in chair
And there and then
You're weighed in, and there
Into your mouth thermometer placed
And you're one of the faceless.
Though you did have a face!

Now to the ward you're ushered
To see prone figures around
And that's what you'll be
Some are sitting up
And visitors depart,
But you've got no one
You're new, just part

Of the incoming stream
Though just caught round a rock
There will you stay, for clothes gone, even frock
Visitors now going, with cheery "goodbye".

Some sniffing, hankies pressed to their tear-filled eyes
I suppose it is really
They're mightily grieved
But who knows, appearances
Oft do deceive.

Some of them really look furtively round
They're glad they're not you,
They're now homeward bound.
"Now you're undressed, dear"
And settled in bed
But give me the word nurse,
And I'm off home
Sharp – they fled.

Now be so of courage
For what to surmise?
You'll either be recovered
Or face covered – *demise*;
All eggs in one basket,
For what do you know
All around you are Spirits
Like Aunt Sallies in row.
Stuck up with big pillows,
But not raring to go!
Passes the night
The dim wards are still
Then someone calls out
There's a rush all around
That trauma over
A snore, then – no sound!

The next morn the big scene
Garbed in snowy white
You have your pre-med
And that stills you fright
Though you know that your face
Has gone pallid, death white
Rattle of trolley, O Me, and O My
Seems like a procession
You're prone still and sigh
No longer yourself, but a doll on a ledge.

Rattling and banging,
No not yet life has fled
But you're a number, labelled on wrist, known when dead!

Now pounced on, off trolley
On another to ride,
And into oblivion you rapidly glide
What are they doing?
Only they really know
For you're just a body
To be "sliced up" But "NO!"
Could be a wonder?
A miracle wrought
Somehow I don't think

That's just a brave thought
– cheering me up.

It's my turn to cringe
For I'm back in my bed
Looking like beer on a binge
I see now a ticket
Pinned largely on me
To be posted elsewhere?
No!, I'm here
Panic flee.

There were four in my ward
And we all gazed around
Though I was the last to recover consciousness I found
I had been raising my left hand so high
Perhaps I was signalling
That I didn't die.
When we all felt better
We chatted away
And such sad stories told
I'm lucky, I say.

The next day we're off
Then outpatients be
And the "in" isn't staying
For "out" all are we.
Now Ethel and Vera
Are dressed up to fly
Wish it were my turn
To say cheery "goodbye".
But whilst I lie in, I must be out soon,
Or am I just wishing like the man in the moon.

January 31st 1988

Oh dearie me, what do I see?
A few gaps where
White teeth gleamed so fair,
Is it of "Age"
And turned twice Life's page?

Can't be, not *yet*!
Most parts can get
Perhaps wooden legs and such-like as these
And a few embellishments added to please
But give a wide smile
And shocked friends to be
When partly I'm toothless
And those there, they can't see,
Most of my teeth are straight, strong and sharp
Just a few at the front
Now on these I must harp.
To tell the truth, I'm really far from happy
And I fled to the dentist
Really put out and snappy.

"*Now* what you need," said he, "is a plate!"
"But we've got stacks of those in the cupboard," my mate
Meaning my husband – will say.
"Good grief not any more
Bring in owt else and we'll be pushed out of door."

"Oh no," said the dentist, "a plate to hold teeth."
To replace those gone missing
Then your lips won't fold in
Round your gums underneath!
"Now I'll have a good look"
To the nurse, "Bring the book,
Now! Three molars to right
The same on the left

Repeat now on top
And the eye teeth she's got."

He went on and on, I felt like a sheep
And now for the spaces
I should think, time to weep.
"Now those that *are* there
Shall stand in good stead
Probably keep them until she is dead."
I imagine myself going up in dark smoke
And midst my ashes, the teeth
Frightening the bloke
Who does the furnace, Oh my.
He sure sees some sights when the brethren do die!

Now, to take the impression,
What's this all about?
My mouth stuffed with cement
'Spect the teeth left all come out
Oh!! The ordeal, I nearly did scream
Then he tugged and he puffed
A nightmare, bad dream!
He was just like the giant
Who breathed hard at panto
When out came to rock
Right smartly and pronto,
My teeth still felt in!
But loosened they'd bin
Yank, yank, what a fright
A drop of blood fell
I swooned then with fright.

He patted my head
"Good girl, now my fee."
And he gave me the bill
When my mouth at last free
Another bout of torture.

At a later date
And I gave up ghost, at the prospect of fate
Marking me down for his playful whim
When all I wanted was a few teeth put in.

I attended again, another impression he took
And if my gums were still in
Well! It surprised me, his look
Seemed so cross, pained
And *he* was fine, *me* well!
I couldn't be blamed
For wishing the one who dished out the teeth
Would make them cast iron and rubber underneath
Then the odd teeth went in
When the plate ready were
He showed me in mirror
And I looked most fair
I went to a concert to sing well that night
Bit on a biscuit and broke tooth a right
A Charlie I looked, for oh what a sight
A big space in the centre
And sang I so well
When between notes I hissed
And lisped too, and tell
Do I now, you, an ordeal it was
For I looked like a fish
All gums on a dish
Anyway when back I went
Repaired new teeth lent
Now to continue this sorry tale
Which to the reader sounds one long, big, wail.
Then I got my proper ones
They slid into place
And really quite approved of my new looking face.

Then along came my friend,
Who was most aware

That if she had gaps
My teeth she did care
To have them copied
And would I loan them out
To show her dentist, then he'd know what's about.

Off then she'd gone, my teeth in her bag,
I'd put them in plastic, wrapped up in clean rag!
"Oh my!" said the dentist, "your poor friend, is she toothless,
now you have her teeth that I see?!"
This *is* a spare set, and so he did relax.
And she brought them safely a week later back.
Handed them over, and chuckled with glee
For her dentist would make hers
Match mine then to see

Now teeth on a plate, have a mind of their own
And they're not always friendly with yours that's home grown.
In fact they can argue
But certainly you don't hear
And if they come out (like strikes)
It can cost you dear.
Particularly if company in you be
A loud laugh – they drop down
It's not nice to see.

Then they're most genteel, looking good on sight
That is if you're lucky and they settle in alright
If you've a mouthful, well no problem there
It's either full house, or they're all gone, gums bare.

Such as a sneeze, beware of this please
Or you're thumped on the back
Or you cough give throat ease,
Oh dear, such a bind, when the falsies come in
And the prospect of more
Like trade unions, it's grim.

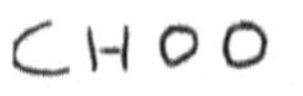

If they are hostile, then settle for none
And show to the world
An expanse of pink gum
Now if you're depressed with all that I've said
Well! Come to the end, I mean when you're dead
I'm quite sure those left
Will vouch for my words
You will depart, and no more to be heard (I think!)
What teeth you have left
Will not with you go
And this is a moral I'd like you to know
If you do hear the words
"Now's time to come"
Perhaps a meal's waiting
Well chomp on your gum
And don't forget, time – years back and then
Teeth made of pot were heavy and when
You did depart they could weigh you down
But plastic one's light, could form part of your crown.

When you're well nigh gone
They pinch lungs, kidneys, heart
But they don't grab your teeth,
They leave that part!

Just imagine when all body's dust
Rows of teeth smiling
Good grief, what a crush,
And they'll all be like new
With a scrub, polish, brush!

www.ingramcontent.com/pod-product-compliance
Ingram Content Group UK Ltd.
Pitfield, Milton Keynes, MK11 3LW, UK
UKHW020134250726
13967UKWH00002B/657

9 780995 574700